room for the seventies

edited by Franco Magnani and Rivista dell'arredamento

translated by Jennetta Ford

Studio Vista London

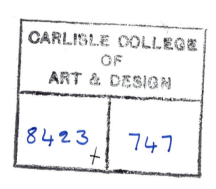
© Görlich Editore S.p.A., Milano 1971
Original edition published in Italy under the title
« Fantasia nell'arredamento »
Edited by Görlich Editore, Milano
Translated into English by Jennetta Ford
Published in Great Britain by Studio Vista
Blue Star House, Highgate Hill, London N19
Made and printed in Italy
ISBN 0 289 70233 X

INTRODUCTION

Everything which surrounds us in our home forms part of its interior decoration; and whether it be a permanent fixture or a movable piece, it has shape and colour. The degree to which each object is pleasing to the eye, the care with which it is chosen, the harmony achieved by the whole will vary in different homes. But the shape and colour of our furnishings are very important, for we live with these objects every day. Their colour and form express and influence our personal taste, our personality, even our ways of thinking.

We cannot live without colour. The very thought of a world in grey is absurd. The importance of colour in interior decoration is therefore obvious, and the relationship of one colour both to form and to other colours has become a matter for detailed study. Any colour, however beautiful in its own right, can be negated or unpleasantly exaggerated if seen in proximity with certain other colours. One's choice is also extremely subjective (there are people who loathe violet, others who detest red) and it may also be dictated by practical considerations: bright paints suit a kitchen because they suggest cleanliness and order, white paint in a nursery would too quickly become dirty. Pale, indefinite colours can acquire a new and interesting emphasis if placed next to a single bright colour, if all of them are chosen with care.

Rules concerning the choice of colour are many and conflicting. Basically this choice will remain a matter of personal taste. But the fact that colour and form are mentioned together presupposes some relationship between these two very elements: different because shape, conceived in the mind of man, is then formed by the hand and has a tactile value, whereas colour has a purely visual appeal.

Architects, designers and interior decorators are constantly trying to discover more about the integration of form and colour, to invent new forms, new colours with which to enhance our houses, make them more welcoming. The intention of this book is to help the reader understand the problem and its solution by proposing many new and exciting answers to the arrangement of the home.

summary

the living room

In the homes of today more space is allotted to the living room than to any other part of the house, for this room is used for so many and different purposes. Consequently, if possible, living rooms should be large, well-planned and easily subdivided, at least visually, into sections expressive of the purpose for which they are used. This sub-division may be achieved by means of furniture, or by sliding screens.

The living room is the place where family and friends come together. For this reason, although it may have many other practical purposes, it is an area in which appearance and atmosphere are especially important. It is here that the personality and interests of the owner are best reflected. But the living room also covers a wide range of activities: reading, resting, talking, listening to music, for example, and whoever is there is connected with the outside world by a variety of audio-visual means. As the place where a family will congregate, at least once a day, it is the ideal centre of domestic life. It must be comfortable and welcoming to any number of people. It should include an area in which one can converse at ease, an area for meals, an area for books, music or hobbies, and sometimes even an area for study.

It is obvious that an area which has so many different purposes will need careful planning. However, the ever-increasing selection of furniture and furnishing devices available goes a long way towards making reasonable solutions possible. A room may be subdivided in various ways. Different pieces of furniture such as shelves or low cupboards, extendable partitions or sliding doors are the most obvious. The latter have the advantage of forming either a total division of the room into separate entities or a partial screening according to need. A particular area of a room may be stressed by a carpet (classical or modern) which contrasts in colour with the rest of the floor.

Colour in a living room is largely provided by fabrics, curtains and upholstery in particular. The textile industry offers the customer the widest possible range. In making one's choice one must remember that the purpose of a curtain is not solely to screen a window, any more than the fabrics covering chairs are merely a disguise for the padding. The fact that curtains, fabrics, carpets introduce colour into a house needs to be kept uppermost in the mind, for the general tone of a room depends on the deliberate harmony and contrast of the colours used in its decoration.

The choice of curtaining will depend to a certain extent on the size of the window. If the room has large picture windows, curtains made of a transparent material could be used during the day and replaced by something of a heavier, more opaque weave in the evening. On the other hand, a single curtain of semi-transparent material is quite suitable for smaller windows.

The problem of flooring can be admirably solved with moquettes, which give a cheerful brightness to a room. Otherwise there is a very wide choice of hand-made woollen carpets, modern carpets created by well-known designers for large industries, or classical carpets. The choice depends on one's pocket.

It is worth ending this brief note on the interior decoration of the living room with the reminder that physical well-being is intricately linked with visual well-being: a correct use of shape and colour, of lighting, and of the distribution of space. To achieve this one needs to be able to perceive an atmosphere and reproduce it with imagination. This is a gift not confined to professional designers.

Architects, designers and books can all be consulted for ideas and solutions to the problems of interior decoration, but in the last analysis it is up to the owner of the house to allow his own personality to come through. It is only when this happens that interior designing is really successful.

1

1
Large living room for a house on Lake Michigan. Architects, Meath and Kessler. Height of living room—two floors. On the upper floor, the study, facing down into the main part of the room, towards the large picture window. View of the lake. Furnishings mainly by Knoll.

2

2
A small living room; interior decoration by Mazzucchelli, architect.
A small room may be organised with clean, functional furnishings.
Light Thonet chairs for the dining area. Comfortable divan by Pol-
tronova for relaxation.

3
Detail of a large living room in a country house on Lake Maggiore.
Architect, Claudio Dini. Staircase leading to the dining room, situated
on a raised level above the room, and to the bedrooms. Living room
once again on two levels. Chairs by Cassina.

4
Large living room in a German family house. Architects, Witzemann and Stadelmaier. This large living area is designed round a central fireplace. Italian chairs by Bellini, produced by C & B.

5

5
Detail of a living room furnished by Ennio Ghiggio, architect. Conversation corner formed by the long divan, "Environ one". The low piece of furniture contains Hi-fi equipment, gramophone and bar and acts as a division between the conversation corner and the dining area.

6
Living room in a flat. Interior decoration by Pini and Zerbi, architects. In the foreground, the dining area. In the background, behind the divan, a small study area. Moquette carpeting; walls covered with fabric.

7

7
Living room in the Guggenheim home at Palazzo Venier dei Leoni, Venice. Living room formed by two linking rooms, with an inter-connecting space from floor to ceiling. The fireplace is behind the division. Paintings on the walls are part of the famous Guggenheim collection.

8
Living area in a recently restored Venetian Palace. Design, Anna Bozza-Coll. Study, Zanipolo. Divans re-covered in sail cloth. Table in fibre-glass with steel supports.

9

9
Study-living room for a collector. Architects, Salvati and Tresoldi. Canvases and sculpture judiciously arranged. The lighting is hidden by wood panelling.

10
Living room for a collector. Interior decoration by Gae Aulenti, architect. The spaces beneath the windows have been designed to hold a valuable collection of seventeenth-century plates. Divans in black leather by C & B. Table in white marble by Knoll.

11
A small but comfortable living room. Designer, Gabriele Basilico. The two low pieces of furniture in the foreground, and the television, separate the dining area from the rest of the room.

10
11

12
Living room for a young couple. Gianfranco Pagliettini, architect. The décor results from a combination of simplicity, taste and a precise sense of colour. The divan—polystyrene cubes, covered with fabric by Meraklon; metal bookshelves by Lips-Vago. The open cupboard spaces at the back of the room are made from painted wood. A clear example of how to achieve a pleasant room without great expense.

13

13
Detail of a living room in a country house. Architects, Anna and Antonello Nuzzo. The divan occupies a predetermined place, fixed to the wall. The small cupboards and prints on the wall form a graceful, though somewhat rigid, composition.

14
Detail of a large living room. Interior decoration by Franco Bartoccini, architect. The conversation corner furnished with divans by Poltronova. Large Klein picture on the wall. A low piece of furniture, serving as cupboard space, runs along the walls.

15

15
Large living room on the top floor. Architect, F. Tartaglia. The area for relaxation is near the large hearth. Seats by Breuer and easy chairs by Eames. Table in the background by Saarinen, produced by Knoll.

the dining area

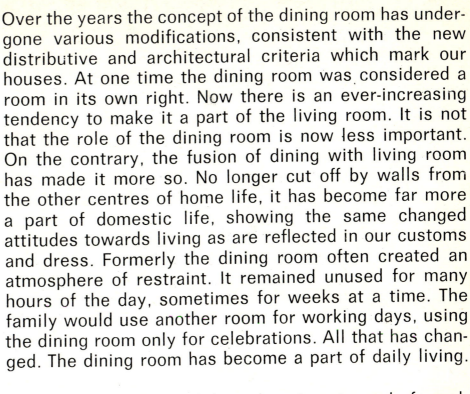

Over the years the concept of the dining room has undergone various modifications, consistent with the new distributive and architectural criteria which mark our houses. At one time the dining room was considered a room in its own right. Now there is an ever-increasing tendency to make it a part of the living room. It is not that the role of the dining room is now less important. On the contrary, the fusion of dining with living room has made it more so. No longer cut off by walls from the other centres of home life, it has become far more a part of domestic life, showing the same changed attitudes towards living as are reflected in our customs and dress. Formerly the dining room often created an atmosphere of restraint. It remained unused for many hours of the day, sometimes for weeks at a time. The family would use another room for working days, using the dining room only for celebrations. All that has changed. The dining room has become a part of daily living.

The change which has taken place is not purely formal. It expresses a new conception: entertaining guests, talking, eating are all a part of domestic life.

Only a few items of furniture are needed in this area: a table, different types of chairs, and a trolley or side-board.

The shape and size of the table will depend on the size of the family and the space available. One should be able to increase its size at will, but this is no problem. Almost all tables manufactured today are provided with side-flaps or some other means of extension. As far as the shape is concerned, the round table is a better buy. The lack of sharp corners is more convenient and adapts more easily to any room. A rectangular table is suitable for a separate dining room, and where there is a space problem, one end may be pushed against the wall.

In most cases dining furniture is sold as a suite, but if one has to choose the pieces individually, these must be in the same style. A modern table usually needs modern chairs to go with it, while antique furniture is better if of the same period and design. There are a few chairs which may be used in any surroundings. This is true of the Chiavari designs, noted for their lightness and elegance, the classic Thonet lines and simple rush-seated chairs in natural wood.

The trolley or sideboard is another indispensable part of the dining room suite. It may be used for the crockery and cutlery, and should have room for additional courses. If on wheels, it may even be used as a conveyance between the dining room and kitchen.

1

1
The dining area in a house in Rome. Design, Studio G. S. Stefano
Mantovani. Dining table in perspex and crystal. Seats by Gavina.
On the wall, a painting by Gaio Visconti. On the table, sculpture
by Beverly Peppers.

2

2
Dining room in a large house in Portofino. Architect, Ezio Sgrelli. The ceiling beams radiate from a wooden pillar and extend to the walls. Mahogany table. Chairs part of the dining suite.

3
Dining area for a country house. Architects, Anna and Antonello Nuzzo. The area is surrounded by small cupboards by Poltronova. Table by Kartell. Lamp made in Finland.

4
Dining area with interior decoration by Pini and Zerbi, architects. Walls covered in material the same colour as the moquette carpeting, so that walls and floor harmonise to provide a background for the furniture. Walnut ceiling.

3

4

5

5
Dining area on the top floor; interior decoration by F. Tartaglia, architect. The area is divided off from the rest of the room by low cupboards. Table in steel and glass by Gavina. Chairs by Eames.

6
Dining corner in a room with interior decoration by G. Ausenda, architect. It is situated in the middle of a large living area, screened from the room with translucent perspex. Lighting projected on to the screen through a mobile complex. Table by Ny Form.

7

7
Dining area in a flat. Interior decoration by Salvati and Tresoldi, architects. Table and cupboards form a single piece of furniture. Sculpture by Gio Pomodoro.

the kitchen

The design of a modern kitchen must take two important factors into account. Although the room has a practical purpose and should be arranged in order to make the work easier, its appearance should nevertheless be as attractive as possible.

The tendency of modern design has been to incorporate essential kitchen items such as the oven and refrigerator into a harmonious relationship with the remainder of the furnishing. Because of the reduced size of the average kitchen, the layout must be carefully considered.

In a well conceived kitchen the various implements and pieces of furniture must be arranged to allow for perfect organisation of work. If this is planned rationally, movement is cut to a minimum and the various spheres of activity are kept separate, avoiding confusion of labour. The work may be divided into three different stages of activity: preparation of food, cooking and washing up.

A large surface area is the first essential for the preparation of food. In order to save time and energy, this should be placed as close as possible to the refrigerator and larder. Since food is cooked in the oven, this also should be reasonably near the area of preparation. The same principles should be used in arranging the part of the kitchen used for washing-up dual sinks for washing up and rinsing, a draining board and a drying rack on the wall above. If these things are observed, working conditions and efficiency will be greatly improved.

Colour should be used with moderation in a kitchen. If a strong shade, such as red, is chosen, the neighbouring colours should be much reduced. White is unsuitable since so much crockery is also white. As much of the furniture is made of wood, a kitchen's natural warmth will be best enhanced by warm, gentle colours.

It must be remembered that interior design does not only involve the question of furniture. It is a complex of every element in the room, and if one wishes the kitchen to be as welcoming as the rest of the house, the rigid functionality of cooking devices must be countered. In the old days the welcoming warmth of a kitchen was created by the open fire. And even if the fire has been replaced by the anonymous blue gas flame, it is still possible to retain something of that original atmosphere.

1

1
Small kitchen directly connected with the living room in a
mountain flat. Interior decoration by Piero Menichetti. Walls in
ceramic tiles and wood.

2

Detail of a kitchen with interior decoration by Ferrari and Martano, architects. Note the bench-table for breakfast. Walls entirely covered in ceramic tiles.

3

A particularly interesting design for a kitchen in a flat in the mountains: a central block contains sink, stove and everything necessary for food preparation. Architects, Antonio and Enrico Astori.

4

4
Kitchen of German design. The various items of furniture are chosen and arranged in order to make the maximum use of space. The cupboards have electric sockets for domestic fittings.

5
Large kitchen in a country house. Architect, Alberto Colombi. The working area divides the breakfast room from the area where food is prepared.

6

6
An efficient, if somewhat cold, kitchen. Furnishings by Boffi, in the
"E 5" series. Interior decoration of the flat by G. Ausenda, architect.

7
Small kitchen with interior decoration by Ennio Ghiggio, architect.
In order to save space, lighting fitments are incorporated in a
hanging cupboard. Breakfast table ash with a formica surface.

8
A small, efficient kitchen from a design by Mario Bellini. Walls
entirely in formica. Handles and working surfaces in wood.

the bathroom

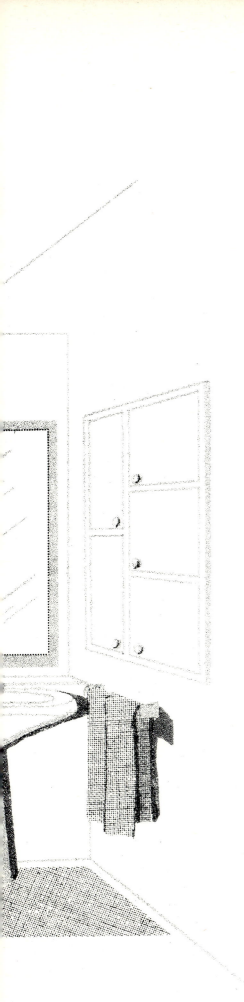

The size and shape of the bathroom is determined by many factors, both economical and practical. And in the cheaper flats of today bathroom space is invariably reduced. It may consist of one room, or of two inter-connecting rooms — one containing bath, handbasin and shower, the other bidet and lavatory. Many modern houses are equipped with a small ante-chamber to the bathroom as well: a space which, suitably furnished and possibly provided with a second handbasin, serves as a dressing room.

Modern bathroom equipment is a great help to interior decoration. Its lines are smooth and elegant, and its colour clean and sparkling, the invariable white of earlier times now often giving place to softer pastel shades. Bath and basin stand out against a background of ceramic tiles, which sometimes cover the floor and ceiling as well.

Bathroom furniture is not limited to bath, basin and lavatory. It includes such fittings as cupboards, brackets, towel-rails, lights, soap-dishes, all of which are necessary to comfort. Industry is producing an ever-increasing range of such accessories. Plastic articles have contributed greatly to our comfort, replacing wooden accessories which deteriorate quickly in damp heat. And plastic is not only more hygienic, but more colourful.

Interior decoration is just as important in the bathroom as elsewhere in the house. There is no reason why a room should not be beautiful as well as functional.

1

1
Bathroom in an American house. Washbasins and dressing table are combined so that the space can double as a small dressing room.

2

2
An example of a rectangular bathroom, a rather unusual shape, divided by shelving (in which toilet articles may be stored) into bath area and changing area.

3
A bathroom with built-in basins. The positioning of the mirrors has been carefully considered in order to achieve the maximum reflection. The lamps have been built into the ceiling in order to give a uniform light.

4
A small bathroom of awkward shape (a modernised flat in an old building). Architect, Antonio Ornati. A welcoming atmosphere has been achieved by painting both ceiling and walls in the same orange colour. Towel hooks by Thonet. Kartell lights.

5

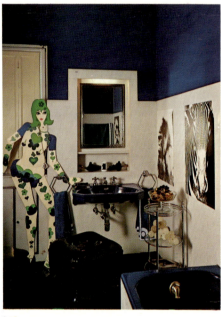

6

5
Small bathroom for children. Made pleasant with brightly coloured wall decoration. Painted wood shelf above the washbasin. In the foreground the shower.

6
An extraordinary effect achieved with a highly individual colour scheme. Ceiling, floor, bath and washbasin all in the same strong colour. The handrail beside the washbasin serves as a towel rail. Studio G. S. Stefano Mantovani.

7
A luxury bathroom by Martine Dufour. Bath, floor and ceiling in onyx. The inside of the bath is satinised steel. Neither a common nor a cheap method of decorating a bathroom, but the example does show how an apparently unfurnishable room like the bathroom may be treated in the same way as all other rooms.

8

9

8
A small bathroom in a flat in the mountains has been "enlarged" by means of a large mirror covering one wall and by use of the tiling design. Designer, Piero Menichetti.

9
Detail of a small bathroom. Interior decoration by Salvati and Tresoldi. An impression of more space is again achieved by the use of mirrors.

the bedroom

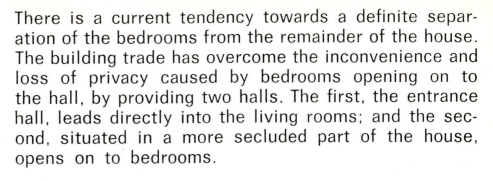

There is a current tendency towards a definite separation of the bedrooms from the remainder of the house. The building trade has overcome the inconvenience and loss of privacy caused by bedrooms opening on to the hall, by providing two halls. The first, the entrance hall, leads directly into the living rooms; and the second, situated in a more secluded part of the house, opens on to bedrooms.

The interior decoration of the bedroom should express intimacy, peace and quiet. Furniture, fabrics and fittings (antique or modern) should be chosen with this in mind. The amount of furniture should be kept to a minimum - a bed, bedside tables, dressing table and wardrobe being all that is necessary. The latter may even be relegated to the dressing room or built into the walls.

The colour in a bedroom will come mainly from the fabrics, and these should be in restful shades such as pale green, blue, deep yellow or ivory. Carpets, particularly if they are fitted from wall to wall, will increase the impression of comfort. If there is a dressing room, the same carpeting may be continued throughout, emphasising the relationship of the two rooms and thus giving a greater sense of continuity.

Double curtains are better in a bedroom, since the degree of light or darkness in the room may then be varied as required. It should be remembered that curtains have an ornamental as well as practical purpose. If carefully designed they will make other decoration superfluous.

A large bedroom has advantages in that it lends itself to unusual arrangements of furniture. For example, a bed may be placed in the centre of the room, thus emphasising its importance. The circular bed was, in fact, the product of just such a concept.

The designer will have most freedom when planning rooms for young people. Many things which an adult might consider too simple or revolutionary will be accepted by younger people with enthusiasm. Moreover, their bedrooms tend to be more than merely places for sleeping. They can be studies, playrooms, living rooms, as well — a small world in which to receive friends, store belongings, work at special interests and hobbies. Complete in themselves, they are used all the time.

1

1
Dressing table with mirror, designed for a modern bedroom by
Antonia Astori.

2

4

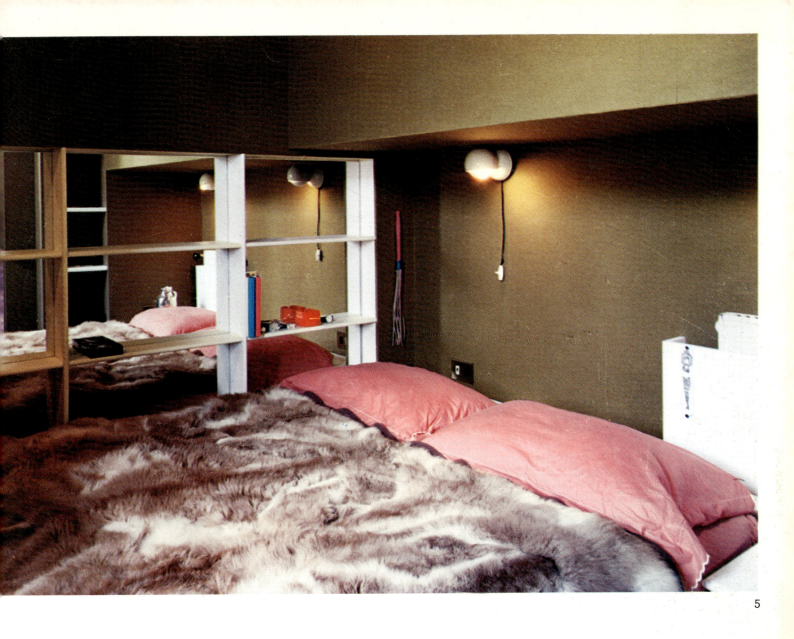

5

2
Bedroom suite including low cupboards and dressing table. Produced in washable formica. Design and production, Vergani.

3
Bedroom suite in lacquered wood. German production.

4
Divan bed in a children's bedroom. Designer, Antonia Astori. Divan is foam rubber on a wooden base. Bed cover in linen.

5
Bedroom in a small flat in the mountains. The shelf unit is placed right against the bed. Behind the shelves is a mirror which gives an impression of more space. Designer, Piero Menichetti.

6
Bed by Interlübke (Germany); wall cupboards by De Padova.

7
An original bedroom with interior decoration by Stefano Mantovani. Bed made of fibre-glass and steel. Table and octagonal lamp in perspex. Collage on the wall by Marina Lante della Rovere.

6

7

8

8
A sensible, simple little bedroom in an American house. Furniture by Knoll. The wall in the background covered entirely with wood panelling.

9

9
Bedroom furnished by a German manufacturer. The bed has a section at the head which may be raised in twelve different positions. Hülsta production.

10
Bedroom suite made in Germany by Hülsta. The items come in different types of wood—walnut, rosewood, ash or oak—and in various colours.

11

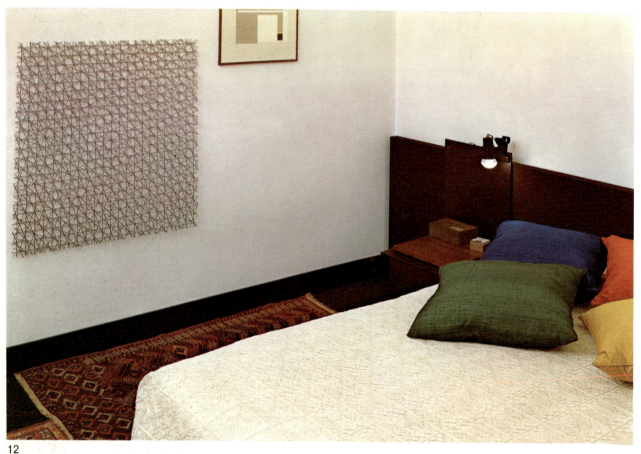

12

11
Small double bedroom in a flat. Interior decoration by D'Urbino and De Pas. The room connects directly with the living room, and can be shut off when necessary by a sliding door, painted green. The bedspread is also green. The bedhead is made from woven ribbon, of a yellow shade.

12
Bedroom in a flat. Interior decoration by Vigano. The bedhead is covered with cloth, and extends to include movable bedside tables. Paintings by L. Morellet.

13
Bedroom for a flat in Venice, Casa Sarasin. Bed designed by Le Corbusier, in steel chrome tubing. On either side are gondola chairs used as bedside tables. The pictures are by Beth Sarasin.

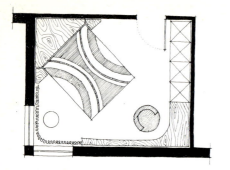

14

14
Double bedroom; interior decoration by A. Astori, architect. Sculpture above the bed by Calvi.

15

15

Study-bedroom for a young man, with a suite made in Germany by Hülsta. The suite has been designed to allow maximum interrelation of the different parts.

16

A modern bedroom. The bedhead is made from yellow and white
painted wood and is fitted with a light. Designer, Ottogalli. The split-
level floor is covered in brown moquette.

17
A simple bedroom with a single bed in expandable polyurethane, covered in white fibre-glass. Red velvet bedspread.

18
Study-bedroom for a boy. Architect, Antonio Ornati. Shelves and working surfaces in solid walnut placed around the walls. Bed in wood, painted white.

17

18

19

Children's bedroom in a country house. Architects, Anna and Antonello Nuzzo. When possible it is an excellent idea to have the play room and bedroom either intercommunicating or forming one room.

the hall

The hall's position in a house varies, but its characteristics are determined by the fact that it is the entrance to the house and therefore has certain fixed uses. Its furnishing depends on whether the hall is linked by a passage to other rooms, or whether the access to other rooms is direct. In the latter case it almost has the function of an ante-room. The size of the hall also determines the extent of its use. If it is very small it probably serves merely as a cloakroom. But a larger space may provide a kind of reception room, thus achieving a greater, if still indefinite, importance.

There are few requirements essential to a hall and most of these, such as hanging space, can be built into the walls. In this way only a few objects protrude and may be chosen for their elegance or particular character. Before we consider such items in detail, the background against which they will take their place must be reviewed.

The walls and floor should be a single colour which will off-set the individual pieces of furniture. The latter can be of modern design, their purpose expressed by their shape. However, if the practical purpose of any particular object is too accentuated, it may prove difficult to place it next to other, less precise pieces of furniture. In a large room the problem is not great because any piece of furniture can be isolated. In a small room all the furniture needs to express the rigidly practical nature of the hall. The dominating effect of strictly practical furniture can be further reduced if cupboards, coat stands and other large pieces are arranged with smaller objects in between.

There are many articles that are designed specifically for use in the hall — some of them, by virtue of their simplicity or practicality, more important than others. The umbrella stand is one of these, though one may, of course, use a large vase or similar container.

Such pieces of furniture as the umbrella stand can introduce patches of colour into a house. The plastic materials can provide them with life and brightness even where they are modern re-interpretations of traditional designs. A hall chest is an example of such a piece of furniture. Although its looks may have changed over the centuries it still retains its original purpose.

There are items of furniture in the modern hall which

are a specific product of modern life. The telephone stand is one — though one can often use a piece of furniture originally designed for a different purpose.

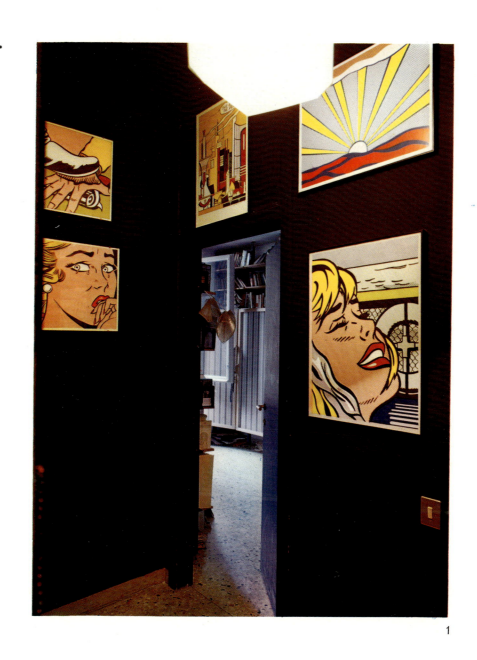

1

1
Hall in the flat of Paolo Barozzi, who owns a gallery in Venice.

2

2
Once again the hall, belonging to a collector in Rome, has been transformed into an exhibition room. On the floor a bronze by Gio Pomodoro. Designer, Carla Panicali.
These are two examples of the use of a room which normally has no particular function: here the space gives great value to the works of art. Even if one is not a collector something of the same effect may be produced with good reproductions.

3

3
The hallway in a flat. Interior decoration by A. Astori, architect. The area is given character by the unusual shaping of the walls and seating, and also by the varying levels of the ceiling. Sculpture by Tavernari.

4

4
Hallway for a house in Rome. Interior decoration by Stefano Mantovani. Sculpture by Gino Marotta.

5

5
In this case, the hall, which is more a long corridor than a room, is directly connected with the living room. The relationship between the two areas is emphasised by the use of the same moquette carpet. Architect, Claudio Dini.

6

6
Another example of a hall which is a part of the living room. The hall is in the background of the photo. The carpeting also extends into a part of the living room. The wooden bench is used as a division between the two areas. Architects, Pini and Zerbi.

7
Small entrance hall, partially connected to the living room. The two spaces are divided by the painted wood partition and by two armchairs (in the foreground). The door on the left, in the foreground, leads into the rest of the flat. Architects, Pini and Zerbi.

8
Small entrance area, screened from the living room by a pillar on the right. Bookshelves by Lips Vago. Floor in natural larch wood. Architect, Patrizio Bedon.

stairs

Stairs within a house have a character which symbolizes movement. Although structurally static, this effect of motion offers a great freedom to the designer. No longer is the staircase merely a means of connecting two floors. It is a fundamental element in the aesthetics of the architectural whole. If the materials are used skilfully, it is possible to achieve truly lyrical results in design.

Banisters no longer exist for the modern staircase. They have been replaced by a rail, a small support in no way intruding on the structure as a whole. In some cases, when it is unnecessary to consider young children or old people, even the rail has been eliminated, leaving the profile of the stairs unadulterated.

The shape of the stairs naturally depends on the surroundings and composition of the framework. There are stairs with steps of wood, stone, crystal, plastic, or some other synthetic material; stairs with vibrant steps, projecting boldly, like wings, from a central axis; hanging stairs, running freely in a void, the girders reduced to mere points of equilibrium supporting them; intricate stairs, born of the desire to find an aesthetic formula expressive of both structure and function.

Such stairways are constructions which reveal to the eye the measured play of tensions and stresses, translated into a physical form. They suggest ease to anyone wishing to climb them.

Reduced to the barest minimum, these skeleton steps express themselves in terms of primary forces. They are a practical element of inter-connection transformed into a decorative fact around which is centred the entire decoration of a room.

1

1
Staircase designed as a piece of sculpture. Architect, L. Galla-
rini. Moquette carpeting; walls in "natural straw" with orange
decoration. The banisters are in dark walnut.

2

2
Stairs in a house in Portofino. Architect, Ezio Sgrelli. Floor and steps
in slate. Handrail in painted iron—this forms the dominant element
of the composition.

3

3
Stairs in a country house. Architects, Morganti and Vender. The stairs are hidden from the living room by a group of furniture and by a screen.

4

Spiral staircase, in prefabricated cement, for a villa in Detroit. Architects, Meath and Kessler. The staircase area is emphasised by the flooring and the lighting.

5

Spiral staircase in metal for an attic flat on two floors. Designer, Luigi Sturchio. A very light composition which fits in easily with the rest of the interior decoration.

4

6

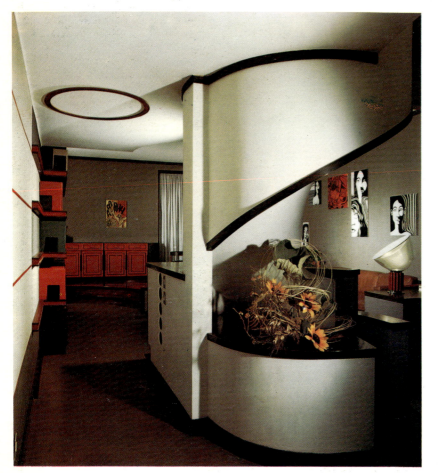

6-7
A spiral staircase set into the wall in a flat redesigned by Ruggiero Marchesi, architect. The design of the staircase mediates between the hall and the living room, and is the focal point of the interior decoration. The walls of the hall echo the curved shape of the stairs.

8
Stairs in polished iron with a resin overlay. Vertical bars, tubing, with the hand rail in red. Architects, D'Urbino and De Pas.

7

9

9
Gaily decorated stairs with the uprights covered in majolica tiling,
designed by the painter Melani. The upper part of the steps in dark
walnut. Interior decoration by Alberto and Diambra Gatti, architects.

the conversation corner

The traditional division of a house into different rooms, each with a set purpose, is rapidly dying out. Designers are becoming increasingly aware of the need for a more flexible organisation of living space.

As has already been stated, it is important to create a living room with an atmosphere of hospitable intimacy. This is best achieved by setting aside a corner or area of the living space for conversation, for reading, resting, relaxing. All that is basically necessary is a sofa or divan, a couple of easy chairs, a low table and a carpet. Shelves for books, with an enclosed section for a radio, gramophone, tape-recorder, or bar, are an additional comfort, and may be easily achieved by means of metal or wooden supports, either placed against the wall, or used as a partition, dividing the corner from the rest of the room.

Lighting is of great importance in helping to create an intimate atmosphere. There are many types of lamp to choose from, whether wall fixtures, standard lamps, ceiling lights or table lamps. The shades may be either of metal or fabric. Excessive dispersion of light should be avoided — sometimes a ceiling light can be directed towards the corner of the room chosen for conversation, so as to create the right atmosphere.

The choice of curtains and other fabrics can also help to create an intimate effect. If the area chosen is near the window, the curtains can provide an additional, decorative element. Modern designs and bright colours go a long way towards giving a room a cheerful atmosphere. The corner chosen for conversation need not necessarily be near the dining area. It might equally be in the hall, bedroom or study. Lack of space in many cases will make such an alternative unavoidable. Nonetheless, a conversation corner is a good idea, a genuine product of modern living.

1

1
A comfortable corner for relaxation furnished with chairs and a divan covered in leather, designed by Buzzi, architect. In this room the plants are of great importance for the contrast they provide.

3

2

2
A large bench with two seats, made from coloured fibre-glass. Designed by Cresti and Piazzesi; production, Cucine Gandi

3
A comfortable area for relaxation and conversation, furnished with several divans and low shelves and cupboards. Interior decoration by G. Cesari, architect.

4
"Mito" is a divan which can be assembled in various ways. Together the units provide a comfortable and flexible area for relaxation. Designer, Gjilla Giani; production, Colzani Salotti.

5

5
The conversation corner in this vast room, designed by Vittorio Introini, is formed from two upholstered divans by Saporiti. Between the two divans, the Flos lamp, designed by Castiglioni.

6
Conversation area in a room designed by Pini and Zerbi, architects. The divans, by C & B, form a quiet corner for relaxation. The corner is partially separated from the rest of the room by a light screen on the right.

7

7
The conversation corner in a large living room in a house in Rome.
Architect, A. Malvasi. The tufa walls give the room a rustic air,
which is well suited to the traditional design of the comfortable
divans.

fires

In our modern apartments, with their efficient central heating systems, the role of the fire and fireplace has become more decorative than practical. Yet a fire is still symbolic of that atmosphere of family intimacy one is trying to create.

There are many types and designs for the modern room. A fire may be built into a corner, set flush with the wall without a chimney piece or, like a stove, totally detached from the wall. Its position should be chosen with a view to emphasising a particular area where people group themselves, since nowadays the main purpose of a fire is this rather than the distribution of heat. Consequently, although one finds fireplaces in many living rooms, they do not exist so much in other parts of the house as they used to do.

Since, in the main, the heating function of the fire is not so important, the decorative element of the fireplace needs a greater degree of attention. The most practical type of fireplace is simple, rectangular in shape and partially inserted into the wall with only the square hearth visible. The hearth can then be emphasised simply in stone or marble, in a contrasting colour to that of the wall. The importance of the hearth can be enhanced by leaving the adjacent walls bare, or by covering them with bookshelves. The latter solution is more suitable for small rooms, whereas in large rooms it may be better to position table and bench surfaces along the wall, and so provide a feeling of greater comfort.

The look of every type of fire, whatever the materials used for the fireplace, depends on the juxtapositioning of materials, and thus on the results of research for original shapes suitable for it, which will make it stand out from the other furniture and become the focal point of attention. New developments in material and colour are nowadays providing a whole series of details more or less connected with the fireplace itself. There are also many new accessories being designed for the fireplace sorround, quite apart from such furniture as is chosen to emphasise and qualify the shape of the hearth.

1
Small fireplace in an American house. Architects, Meath and Kessler. A small conversation corner has been created around the fireplace with comfortable divans.

2

2
A fireplace of an unusual circular design in a country house. Interior decoration by Antonio Piva, architect.

3
Fireplace in beaten iron for a house in the mountains. It is suspended from the ceiling. The base of the fire is brickwork. Architects, Antonia and Enrico Astori.

4
Fireplace in cement for a country house. The fireplace is the focal point around which the room is designed. Architect, Alberto Colombo.

5

5
Small majolica fireplace in a Venetian flat, Casa Sarasin at Zattere.
The mirror is of the same period.

6
Large fireplace in a country house. Interior decoration by Diambra
Gatti, architect. The mantelpiece has been used for a collection of
fossils.

6

7
Example of a fireplace which is inserted completely into the wall. Room furnished by A. Astori, architect. The bookshelves and cupboards are built into the same wall. Above the fireplace a picture by M. Marini.

book cases

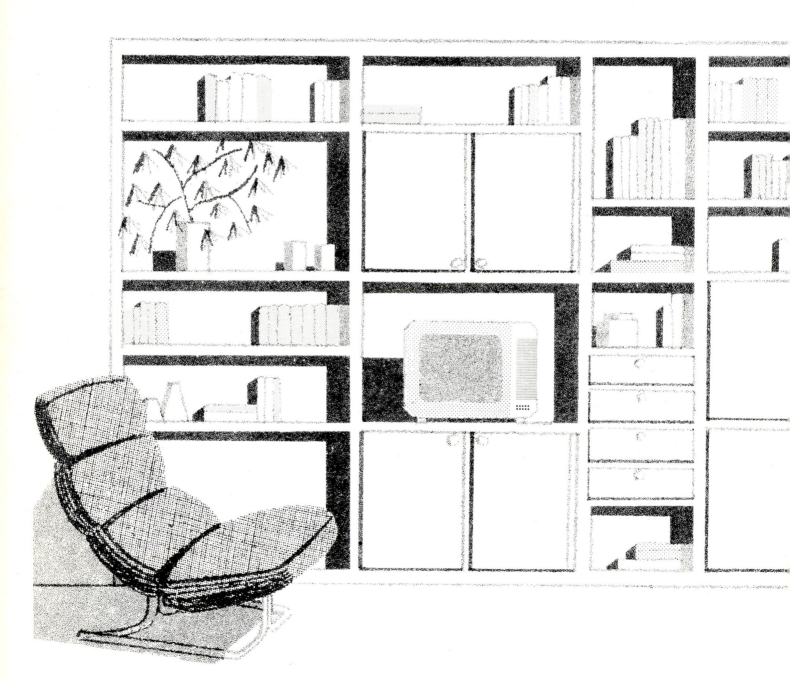

Book cases and shelves are not used only for books. They are also ideal for collectors' pieces. And who does not have treasures in his house which he wants to display? Who is not, to some extent, a collector? One does not have to be rich to own antiques. In most homes there are books and ornaments, collected over the years, which the owner would never part with. There may be collections of paintings, porcelain, sculpture by important artists, rare books, or exotic mementoes collected in faraway lands — hunting trophies, primitive weapons, tribal masks. A nature lover will have curious stones, butterflies, shells, or fossils of various kinds, and most houses contain family possessions, handed down through generations, no longer in general use, but no less important to the owner for that. Whatever the particular collections may be, they can, if properly displayed together with books, enrich and add personality to the furnishing of a room.

There are infinite possibilities in the way of shelves for such things. Bracket shelves, glass-fronted cases and bookcases are the most usual, but in every home there is some nook or cranny ideal for a particular item or book.

In themselves, books are the most colourful, lively and changeable items in a room. They are also an easy means of creating an effect of warmth. Whether they are precious first editions or paperbacks piled in odd corners, they brighten the atmosphere.

Even in a small house the need to provide space for books is not necessarily a disadvantage, since they are then handy for reference as well as providing points of attraction. The arrangement should, however, be considered carefully in the first place so that each item or object achieves its maximum effect.

If a large wall is available, the best way to display any object is to place it on bookshelves covering perhaps the entire wall. Such shelves can also provide space for a bar, gramophone or television. Living today presents new problems in interior decoration because of the need for objects such as these, but with thought one can find many solutions.

1

1
This beautiful bookcase of steel and wood is placed along the wall of a long corridor. Restoration of a Venetian palace, Anna Bozza, Studio Zanipolo.

2

2
Low cupboard which also serves as a bookcase, placed as a partition in a living room with interior decoration by Ferrari and Martano, architects.

3
Bookcase in wood, going right up to the ceiling, used as a partition. Created from various separate pieces designed as a series. Interior decoration of this Milanese flat by Vittoriano Viganò, architect.

3

4
A low bookcase in a
living room designed by
Pini and Zerbi. The shel-
ves also include the
loudspeakers for the Hi-fi
equipment.

5

5
Painted metal bookshelves, designed by Lips Vago. Placed in a bedroom. Interior decoration by Claudio Dini, architect.

6
Example of a bookcase which covers the entire wall. It is built up from separate pieces, produced by Frangi. Small chairs by Le Corbusier, produced by Cassina. Interior design by Antonio Ornati, architect.

6

7

Wall bookshelves in a design by Forges Davanzati and Ranzani, architects. The bold play of colours is the interesting point in this room.

the study

The place where one reads, listens or writes, the study can be a separate room, or a corner of the living room.

It is no longer possible to think only in terms of a traditional library, with its shelves of books, largely because the material which we study has been extended far beyond the traditional medium. Negatives, films, magnetic tapes, records — all these have to be stored and filed, a problem that needs to be considered more and more nowadays when a house is being planned. A definite room or corner for this purpose is essential, particularly if there are young people studying in the house.

Students obviously most need the use of a study, whether they rent rooms near their college, or build up a corner in their parents' house. Many rented rooms reveal a self-assured creative capacity, typical of young people, which produces excellent interior design. Simple tables made from a flat working surface, support by two trestles, practical lights with shades which can be altered to direct the beam, book shelves made from a few planks, brightly coloured and nailed to the walls, can all be attractive. No matter how modest one's means, students have proved that one can furnish a place of one's own with taste and intelligence — also using pieces of furniture, already in one's possession, in a new way or for a new purpose. These 'spontaneous' rooms are, indeed, the most attractive studies, for every object has its own **raison d'être**, a combination of practical necessity and personal taste.

The study of a professional man is influenced by other considerations — elegance, comfort and a capacity to reflect the owner's personality or job. Comfortable easy chairs, graceful colours and fabrics, ornaments or pictures reflecting the owner's taste need to be the key note, since the atmosphere these things provide helps to establish a good relationship between visitor and host.

1
A small study in a flat designed by Claudio Dini, architect. The writing desk, cupboard and divan-bed are made of wood, painted white.

2

2
A small study area in a bedroom, with a simple trestle table and a
bookcase reaching up to the ceiling.

3
Studio flat for three young students, economically and imaginatively designed. Simple trestle tables, chairs from a suite, simple shelving in bright colours. Note the adjustable lighting.

4
Small study area which could be created any-
where. Simple wood shelving with a brightly
coloured background. Detail of a design by Paolo
Riani, architect.

5
Study area forming part of the living room. In
Paolo Barozzi's flat in Venice. Once again the
problem is solved with a trestle table, two chairs
and a few cupboards.

4

6

6
A doctor's study. Design by P. De Amicis, architect. Divan designed
by Scarpa, produced by Gavina. Easy chairs by Eames.

7
Study in a country home, designed by Alberto Colombo, architect.
Walls lined with cupboards and shelves, produced by De Padova.

8

8
Living room-cum-study, designed by R. Raimondi, architect. Bookshelves and writing table created from "System Abstracta", by Ponteur. Panels in formica. Walls covered in expandable polyurethane Moquette carpet.

paintings and sculpture

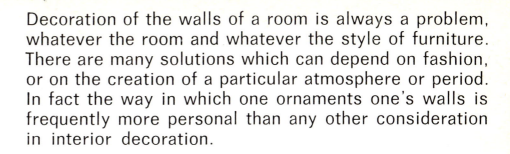

Decoration of the walls of a room is always a problem, whatever the room and whatever the style of furniture. There are many solutions which can depend on fashion, or on the creation of a particular atmosphere or period. In fact the way in which one ornaments one's walls is frequently more personal than any other consideration in interior decoration.

In earlier times the most precise rules, dictated by fashionable tastes and techniques, governed the way in which walls were hung. Until the seventeenth century, for example, frescoes were the most common form of decoration; they covered walls and even ceilings, and depicted legendary or historical events. In the seventeenth century wall-hangings took over, such as the famous Gobelin tapestries in French palaces and the homes of wealthy nobles. **Boiserie**, used previously only in isolated incidences, was the main mood of the eighteenth century; while in the nineteenth century, with the rising importance of the bourgeoisie, the new **papier peint** came into its own, bringing wallpapers whose designs were simple, in comparison with those of the hangings of previous epochs, and placed more weight on freedom and spontaneity.

The different customs and tendencies of previous ages are still present today, for many are integrated into the modern home. The twentieth century has adopted the best elements of most earlier customs, imitating or adapting them, with modern techniques of reproduction, to a modern situation.

Pictures, sculptures or prints are the best wall-decoration for modern houses, since they only take up a part of the wall space. But they can be selected either for their intrinsic value to the owner or for their capacity to fit in with the decoration as a whole. In the latter circumstance, pictures or sculpture can be hung or placed so as to emphasise the type and colour of the wallpaper, and change the composition of the room and the relationships of furniture, doors, chairs, windows. An approach like this is probably advisable for anterooms such as the hall, although works of art hung there may give too great an emphasis to the hall as a room, and thus prints or other objects revealing a certain regularity could be better in a hall.

Prints, when they are used in the way described, are suitable as decoration for almost any type of room, for they fit in easily with most types of furniture, or can stand, convincingly, by themselves. There will be times, however, when one wants the picture or piece of sculpture to take precedence, and the rest of the furnishings to be simplified in contrast. In that case, the wall contouring should be chosen to provide a background, with the lighting adapted accordingly, and the furniture may even be arranged to leave room for people to look at the work or works of art. Corridors are ideally suited to this kind of scheme, for there the objects may be exhibited and viewed with ease.

1

1
A good painting creates a bright spot in any part of the house.
Here it is placed in a passage, with the dark walls making an
excellent background for the picture by Enrico Baj. Design by
Salvati and Tresoldi, architects.

2

3

4

2
Apartment in Milan. Interior decoration by Vittorino Viganò, architect. Paintings by Fontana and Munari.

3-4
In these examples the geometric compositions dominate the space. Collage and sculpture by Giglioli, furniture by Knoll.

5
Relationship between a modern tapestry and a period bronze. The realism of the bronze and the tones of the tapestry create an atmosphere of magic, in which the rest of the furniture serves a complementary purpose. Composition photographed by Galleria Beurdeley. Tapestry by J. Alberif; statue of Buddha is fourteenth century.

7

6

6
The abstract is a dark, severe note in the room. Interior decoration by Pini and Zerbi. Abstract by Paola Frasconi.

7
Collector's living room. Architects, Salvati and Tresoldi. The colour of the walls, furniture and floor creates a warm and uniform atmosphere which gives the paintings their full value. Works by Corpora, Bryen, Messager, Scanavino.

8
Another example of a room where modern works of art are harmoniously combined with antique furniture. Design by Luigi Sturchio. Abstracts by Valentino Dionisi.

8

9
The strength of the painting in the background would overwhelm the rest of the furnishings if it were not for the plate of fruit, which provides a refreshing balance. Tapestry by Atlan. Interior decoration by Hermann Miller. Photo by Mobilier International, Paris.

10

10
Once again the uniform tones of the walls, floor and upholstery provide a background, this time for the two paintings by Ormenese and Palma.

11

11
Tapestry by Eudaldo. Sculpture by Giglioli. Spanish period table.
Modern furnishings by Miller. Architect, Novarino.

indoor sports

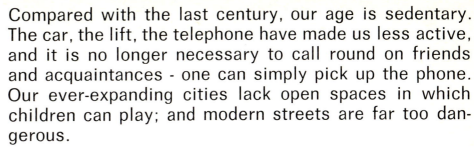

Compared with the last century, our age is sedentary. The car, the lift, the telephone have made us less active, and it is no longer necessary to call round on friends and acquaintances - one can simply pick up the phone. Our ever-expanding cities lack open spaces in which children can play; and modern streets are far too dangerous.

On the other hand, the very things that make our lives more inactive make it possible for a greater section of the population to indulge in some kind of sport. The standard of living is better, which gives the average man more free time. Many more people have a second house in the country. We eat more - and gain tyres of superfluous fat. Consequently we need to learn to exercise our muscles, whether it be in our homes or streets.

With careful organisation, even the smallest house has room for some type of sport. A plan on one of the following pages shows an ideal method for arranging a dartboard. The boy's room has been divided by means of cupboards, so as to leave a central corridor for the game. At the same time this division gives a greater individuality to both sections of the room, where the beds are placed. The subdivision enriches the interior decoration, the dartboard in itself becoming an ornamental feature.

Another of the following plans illustrates a special corner that has been set aside for exercises. Yet another illustrates a room where the equipment used for exercise does not have to be hidden away during the day. The colours of the furniture tone in with the articles used for sport; this all provides an unusual corner for many different activities. The way in which the space is organised is obvious from the sketch. The cupboard divides the room into two different areas. The bed is isolated — though not hidden — in a corner of the room. Consequently, although it is still linked with the room by light and sound, these are muted. Although this solution is most suitable for the summer months, it is nevertheless functional throughout the year.

Yet another sketch suggests a practical use of the hallway in a mountain dwelling, with skis placed against the walls, and covered by plastic carriers when not in use, and with the rest of the décor centred on them, surrounding them with gay, cheerful colours. Basically this solution makes valid use of a space otherwise lost, which is a consideration that makes for comfort.

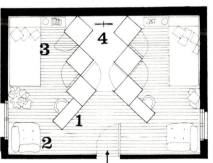

1

1
Shooting target for a boy's bedroom.
Key to the sketch
1 study area   2 sitting area   3 bed   4 sport

2

2
Key to the sketch
1 study area   2 bed and dressing area
3 sitting area   4 sport

3
Key to the sketch
1 study area   2 bed and dressing area
3 sitting area   4 sport

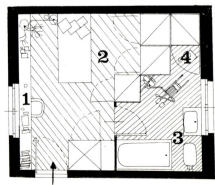

4
Fixtures for skis in a flat in the mountains.
Key to the sketch
1 hallway   2 fixtures for skis   3 living room   4 kitchen

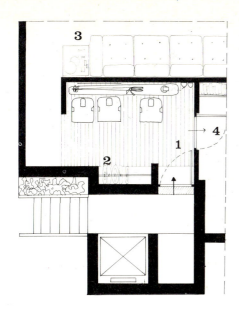

5

6

5
Cupboard designed to hold fishing equipment.

6
Ping-pong table in boy's room. When not in use it can be hung on hooks against the wall.

177

7

7
Perspex cupboard for deep sea diving apparatus. Could be used as
a dividing screen in the living room of a house by the sea.

8
An attic can be used for storing sports equipment. The result here
is a gay wall decoration.

9
A welcoming and pleasant corner set aside for sport.

comfort in the open air

City life has become more and more unnatural to man, as towns grow. Man tends to become estranged from his natural surroundings, and is beginning to show the need once more for the countryside. Even in the centre of a city men will try to create a little space of green, representing the country which is all too often felt to be a lost world. Most residential areas have their little plots of grass and shrubs, pathetic in their surroundings — a confused medley of cement, concrete and asphalt, bordering every road.

Most municipalities attempt to maintain green areas in towns. But — more than this — a much geater importance is being placed on terraces and gardens attached to private dwellings — and, alas, these are still far too few in number, far too small and confined to allow any real sense of being in the open air. Nevertheless even a small strip of green outside one's window is a psychological benefit which allows one a slight relaxation from tension, a confirmation of the existence of the now distant, natural world.

The terraces in a city must have some vegetation, and even if this means that at times in the year they will look bare, this has its own importance. After all, these areas are supposed to reflect nature and the variety of its changes over the course of the seasons.

When planning living spaces in the open air, it is particularly important to give them a personal character, since these constitute the immediate view from one's windows. One's design for terrace or garden should depend on the type of interior decoration one has used in the house. The two extremes of choice outside are probably: an area that is emphatically rustic with an apparently spontaneous vegetation, in which one can perhaps place **chaises-longues** and garden tables, or a neatly planned and carefully kept section, perhaps divided into sub-sections for various activities. The latter is more suited to a small area of garden.

A piece of cane or iron trelliswork covered with climbing plants often suits the rustic atmosphere described above, whereas a partial roof of larchwood or cement is more appropriate to the neater more elegant scheme. Sometimes, of course, the problem has already been solved because the original design of the house included a terrace.

Vertical screens against the wind may be made from fabric, or sheets of glass, and these can be important in an outdoor area used for practical purposes, such as meals. In the right season an outdoor meal can be a very pleasant change, giving a new vitality to a day or evening.

Since out-of-door meals are such a pleasure, it's worth remembering the following: the place reserved for eating should not be too far away from the kitchen; a sunshade is often essential for daytime use, and sufficient lighting must be arranged for the evening.

An outdoor eating area will require appropriate furniture, which may be chosen from classic designs in lacquered metal, or from more simple wood or canework ranges. A stand would be useful to provide additional space for vases of flowers and, if there is sufficient room, a barbecue is, of course, ideal for a meal on the terrace or in the garden.

One point needs to be re-emphasised: the inter-relationship between the external living area and the internal decoration of the house is very important, for besides defining the close relationship between the two areas, it will add an air of completion to both. Particularly helpful here are large glass windows, since they "introduce" the external world to the internal living quarters, and at the same time avoid an abrupt limitation of the external area.

1

1
A terrace designed for a house beside a lake. Furniture—metal
base with wooden cross bars.

2

2
Terrace created as a living room in the open air. Cement flower containers. The sloping roof gives shade to the area.

3
Garden furniture; chairs and table in painted wood with steel supports. Design, Carlo Hauner; produced by Bi Effi Ci.

3

4

4
Collapsible garden chair. Base in painted wood; convering in fabric
or plastic. Design, Carlo Hauner; produced by Reguitti.

5
In this example the outdoor sitting area becomes an ideal contin-
uation of the living room, and is glassed in at the sides.

5

6
This large porchway has been created for a house on the bank of a river, to create space for outdoor living.

7
Metal is excellent for garden furniture. Table and chairs in painted tubular metal, seats in plastic. Table surface in glass. Design G. Carini; produced by Planula.

8
Easy chair with basic structure of plastic-coated steel tubes. Seat in plastic-coated fabric to resist damp and wet. Design G. Frattini; produced by Cassina.